WOLVES

CONTENTS

Original title of book in Spanish:
El Fascinante Mundo de...Los Lobos
© Copyright Parramón Ediciones, S.A.
Published by Parramón Ediciones, S.A., Barcelona, Spain.

Author: Maria Ángels Julivert
Illustrations: Marcel Socías Studios

English text © Copyright 1996 by Barron's Educational
Series, Inc.

All inquiries should be addressed to:
Barron's Educational Series, Inc.
250 Wireless Boulevard
Hauppauge, NY 11788-3917

ISBN: 0-8120-9536-7

Library of Congress Catalog Card No. 95-43049

Library of Congress Cataloging-in-Publication Data

Julivert, Maria Ángels.
  [Fascinante mundo de los lobos. English]
  The fascinating world of—wolves / by Maria Ángels Julivert;
illustrations by Marcel Socías Studios.
    p. cm.
Includes index.
Summary: Describes the habits and habitats of wolves.
  ISBN 0-8120-9536-7
  1. Wolves—Juvenile literature. [1. Wolves] I. Title.
QL737. C22J8513 1996
599.74'442—dc20   95-43049
                                                          CIP
                                                          AC

Printed in Spain
6789 9960 987654321

WOLVES

by
Maria Ángels Julivert

Illustrations by Marcel Socías Studios

BARRON'S

PROFILE OF A HUNTER

T he wolf is an animal that almost always lives in packs. It is a magnificent **predator** with a strong, robust body.

The color of the wolf's fur is varied, with gray the most usual color, although white and even reddish wolves also exist. Its stomach is a lighter shade than its back. It has oval eyes, pointed ears, a long muzzle, and long, sharp teeth. Its legs are long and thin, although they are strong and adapted for running over long distances. It has five toes on its forepaw and four on its hind paw, all with **nonretractable** claws.

An adult measures between 100 and 150 centimeters (40 and 60 inches) long, not including the tail, and weighs between 15 and 80 kilograms (33 and 176 pounds). The male is bigger and heavier than the female. Wolves from cold regions are usually bigger and have longer, thicker fur than wolves from warm regions.

Although we all think we know a lot about wolves, our knowledge owes more to myths and legends than to the facts of this magnificent animal. Its poor reputation does not correspond to the fascinating reality of its social life, language, or hunting techniques.

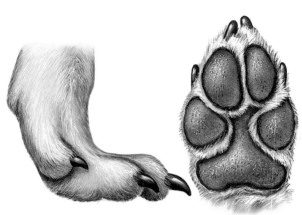

Right: Wolves have pointed ears, a long slim muzzle, and a fur-covered body.

Left: Forepaw of a wolf. The wolf move on its toes.

Left: Silhouettes of a man and a wolf, showing their comparative sizes.

Below: Skeleton of a gray wolf. Like most carnivores it has a strong, agile body.

CARNIVOROUS FOOD SOURCES

A wolf's long, sharp canine teeth and powerful, cutting molars indicate its **carnivorous** diet. A wolf can catch creatures both great and small, although its favorite prey are large herbivores like elk, reindeer, or caribou. All in all, it is an excellent hunter and will catch whatever prey is available in the area in which it lives. For this reason, to find out what the wolves of a specific area feed upon, their excrement, or even the contents of their stomachs, are analyzed. In this way it can be shown that as well as attacking large animals like reindeer or deer, they also hunt roe deer, chamois, boar, beavers, and even small animals like mice, squirrels, rabbits, and hares. Although less common, wolves sometimes even catch birds, reptiles, and insects or, if necessary, eat **carrion**. In autumn they add to their exclusively carnivorous diet with acorns, grapes, or berries.

If wild food is scarce, the wolf will attack farm animals, such as chickens, pigs, cows, sheep, or dogs. The wolf even may make forays in search of food to garbage dumps in areas inhabited by man.

It is calculated that an adult wolf eats between 2 and 4 kilograms (4 ½ and 9 pounds) of meat per day if there is plenty of food available, and in times of scarcity it is capable of devouring much more at once.

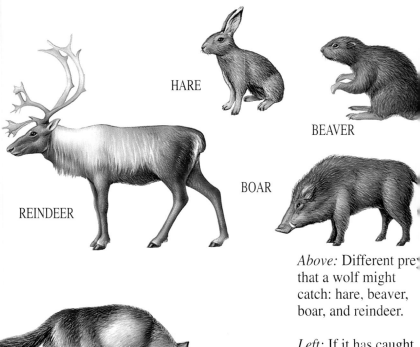

Right: A group of wolves devouring prey.

Above: A wolf's skull in which its grinding molars and carnivorous teeth can be seen.

HARE

BEAVER

BOAR

REINDEER

Above: Different prey that a wolf might catch: hare, beaver, boar, and reindeer.

Left: If it has caught more than one prey, or if the prey is very large, the wolf buries the remains and will return later to finish the feast.

A GREAT PREDATOR

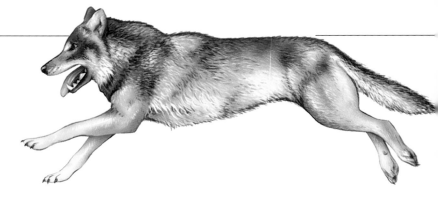

Wolves hunt in groups and maintain this activity throughout the entire year. They are capable of spending the whole night, without a rest, in the hunt for prey. The wolf is a strong, resilient animal that can cover large distances without tiring. Its legs are adapted for running. As it usually hunts in a group, it can bring down animals much larger than itself, such as reindeer, elks, or deer.

Although the wolf is an expert hunter, large prey manage to escape. But this is not the case with the weaker animals, the old, the ill, and the young, which are all easy prey.

The sequence of the hunt is like this: the pack of wolves, guided by the leader, follow the **tracks** of a herd of deer. They close upon the herd silently, with perfect coordination, and when they launch their surprise attack,

they try to separate one of the deer from the rest of the group.

They surround the animal which has fallen behind, depriving it of any means of escape. Then they throw themselves upon it, biting its flanks and stomach until the loss of blood weakens it and it falls to the ground. The hunt has been a success.

In some regions wolves follow herds of wild **herbivores** in their seasonal **migrations**. This is the case in Alaska, where the caribou, in spite of their long trips, have to endure constant attacks from wolves.

Right: An elk pursue by a pack of wolves.

Above: Wolves can run for many kilometers without getting tired.

Below: Wolves attack large animals by bitin the prey until they ar overcome by the wounds to their flank hindquarters, and stomach.

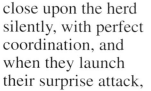

LIFE WITH THE PACK

Right: A pack of wolves resting.

Left: Close-up of a wolf baring its teeth frighten off a fellow wolf.

Below: A wolf in the submissive position, with ears and tail folded and face tense backward, facing another wolf in a dominant position, ta raised, ears erect, an fur standing on end.

T he wolf is a social animal. It lives in groups that are sometimes as large as 40 or as small as 3 or 4. The average is about 10 individuals. The number usually depends on the type of hunting available; in regions where there are plenty of large herbivores, packs are larger in number. For example, on Isle Royale, Michigan, where the main prey is moose, the average number of wolves in a pack is 15 to 20.

All members of the pack participate in hunting, defending their territory, and looking after young. The structure is hierarchical and importance is established by means of combat. It is the law of survival of the fittest. The strongest, or alpha male, is the guide and **leader** of the rest of the group.

In a pack there are two basic ranks, the males and the females. The dominant male and female are the only ones that reproduce and are also the first ones to eat. It is not unusual to see fights among the pack to try and seize the leadership.

Sometimes there exist so-called lone wolves. These are usually young wolves that have been expelled from a pack and wander in search of a place to live. In their search for a mate and a territory, they often cover enormous distances.

TERRITORIES OF THE WOLF

E ach pack of wolves occupies a territory that can stretch for many kilometers and that it defends against incursions from other wolves. The extent of the territory depends principally on the number of individuals making up the pack, the time of the year, and the availability of food.

Wolves mark their territory with urine and excrement. These odors among vegetation or rocks, mark the limits of their territory. They are a warning for other wolves that the area is occupied; in this way they avoid unnecessary confrontations with other groups. Also when they howl, they warn others of their presence, and indicate to the rest of the pack where they are besides.

The pack constantly travels its territory along paths, firebreaks, and streams. The wolves travel in single file behind the leader and often cover long distances in search of food. Between the different territories of each pack there is generally a neutral zone. It is usually an area for so-called lone wolves. Only when there is a great scarcity of hunting will a pack cross into or invade another pack's territory. In this case a fight is inevitable.

Right: Wolves howl to warn others of their presence and to avoid unnecessary fights. To howl they lift their heads to the sky.

Center: Territorial zones occupied by two packs. In the center is no-man's land.

Below: A pack in search of prey can travel up to 100 km (60 miles) in a day.

NO-MAN'S LAND
AREA WITHOUT WOLVES

COMMUNICATION AND LANGUAGE

Wolves are social animals that act in a group and need to communicate with one another. They express their feelings and emotions, such as anxiety, aggressiveness, or submission, by means of a complex system of sounds, facial expressions, and body movements.

As well as their characteristic howl, audible from many kilometers away, they can emit other guttural sounds: snarls, barks, sighs, yawns, cries, yelps, growls, etc.

Yelps are a type of short wail given with a low voice, expressing their dissatisfaction with something they want but cannot get. Barks are sounds that they emit when they are playing or fighting. Growls show anger when they are fighting. Cries are a call for attention.

The weakest wolves of the pack adopt a submissive attitude toward others. They bend their forelegs, lower their head, and keep their tail between their legs or even roll upside down on the ground with their feet in the air in a posture of defenselessness. These signals inhibit the aggressiveness of the other wolves and protect them against attack.

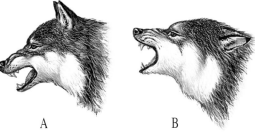

A B

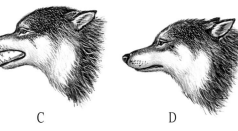

C D

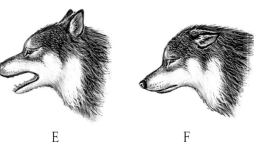

E F

Right: The weaker animal adopts a submissive posture toward the dominant one.

Left: Facial expressions:
A and B: Menacing
C and D: Moderating the threat
E: Relaxing
F: Anxiety.

Below: Expressions with the tail:
1, 2: Dominance
3: Threat from a dominant wolf
4: Threat from a nondominant wolf
5: Indifference
6: Latent threat
7: Anxiety
8: Submission
9: Total submission.

1 2 3 4

5 6 7 8 9

FINDING A DEN

Wolves form stable pairs and reproduce once a year. When females are in heat, fights among the pack are frequent, but the dominant male and female impose themselves on the rest of the pack. Only these two will mate and will have young. Before beginning an attack, a wolf emits a ferocious growl, a low, hoarse sound, accompanied by threatening gestures. In this way it tries to dissuade its opponent and avoid a fight.

Toward the end of winter, the pair separate temporarily from the rest of the pack. When the cubs are a few weeks old they will join the group again. The female searches for a peaceful place to have her young, usually close to a place that has water. She might use the same **den** for several years in a row.

The den is usually a natural cavity, such as a cave, a crevice, a hollow trunk, or a burrow abandoned by another animal. Sometimes they excavate their own refuge themselves. These dens have a simple structure, a hollowed-out chamber in soft earth that has one or more tunnels connecting with the outside.

Right: A wolf coming out from between the roots of a tree, where it has its den.

Right: Wolves show affection by playing and caressing one another.

Below: A wolf positioned at the mouth of a cave.

LOVING PARENTS

Cubs are born after a gestation period lasting about 60 days. They are very small, with dark fur and closed eyes, and are defenseless. The average litter is between four and seven young. During the first few weeks of life the cubs stay in the den with their mother, who looks after them and suckles them. The male is responsible for going hunting and finding food for the mother. When the young wolves are big enough, the parents join the rest of the pack and the cubs' care and protection becomes a task for the whole group.

As the cubs cannot tear and chew meat, the first solid food the cubs eat is **regurgitated** by the adults. The learning period is fairly long. The cubs spend their time playing, chasing and biting one another, and fighting together—imitating the behavior of the adults. During these games not only do they get to know one another and learn, but they also establish the first hierarchies. When the cubs are a little older they will be able to accompany the adults on their hunting expeditions, learning techniques that are vital both for their individual survival and also for the group of which they form a part.

Left: During the first few weeks of life, the main enemies of wolf cubs are the golden eagle and the eagle owl.

Right: The adult wolves feed and protect their cubs and teach them to hunt.

Below: The cubs are born with dark coats, their eyes and auditory canals closed, and their ears flattened down. After 21 days, their ears strengthen and they begin to explore outside the den.

RECENTLY BORN CUB

ONE AND A HALF MONTHS OLD

TWO AND A HALF MONTHS OLD

CANIDAE, A VERY OLD FAMILY

Right: While some researchers consider the wolf to be the predecessor of the domestic dog, others believe it is the predecessor of the jackal.

JACKAL

FOX

HUNTING DOG

DINGO

MANED WOLF

The wolf belongs to the *Canidae* family. The fox, the hunting dog, the coyote, and the maned wolf among others also belong to the same family. Their origin goes back to the Eocene period, more than 40 million years ago, in the geographical region of what is now North America. One of the first members of this old family was the Hesperocyon, although its appearance was more like a present-day mongoose than a dog.

The wolf is the largest of the current *Canidae* and without doubt is one of the most well-known and feared. Coyotes, jackals, and dogs belong to the same genus as the wolf (canis).

There now exist only two species of wolf: the red wolf exclusively in the United States, and the gray wolf, which exists in Europe, Asia, and North America. Thirty-two subspecies of the common wolf have been identified, although some of them are now extinct. In some regions the wolf's situation is precarious and it is in danger of becoming extinct. In many parts of Europe and Asia as well as North America, it has been systematically exterminated because of losses caused to cattle and domestic animals.

WORLD-WIDE HABITATS AND WHITE WOLVES

Left: Dominant male contemplating his lands.

Below: Wolf cubs are born in summer when the climate is relatively mild.

Wolves have managed to adapt themselves to the most diverse of **habitats**. They can be found in forests and mountainous regions as well as steppes, deserts, or the inhospitable tundra. They are distributed throughout Europe, Asia, and North America, and their abundance or scarcity is directly related to the proximity of non-industrialized regions and areas uninhabited by man, their greatest enemy.

The largest wolf populations are found in Alaska, Canada, and Russia. In the Arctic region wolves have longer fur that is lighter-colored, sometimes even white. This subspecies of wolf is distributed in the coldest regions of Eurasia and America: Siberia, Finland, the western islands of Greenland,

Alaska, Canada, the Hudson Bay, and along the Mackenzie River. In the icy tundra their usual prey are elk, caribou, and musk oxen.

A numerous group of arctic wolves lives on Ellesmere Island in the Arctic Circle. This is a subspecies perfectly adapted to harsh climatic conditions. The young are born in summer and the adults catch hares, lemmings, seagulls, and musk oxen. Although their behavior and customs are similar to the rest of their relatives, they have the good fortune to live in practically unspoiled land with no human population.

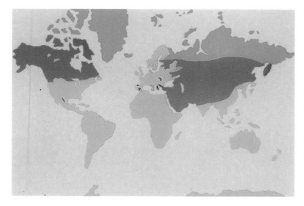

Right: The white wolf has been able to adapt itself to the most severe environmental conditions.

Left: Map ■ of the distribution of wolves in the world.

■ Distribution of the three subspecies of white wolf.

THE AMERICAN SUBSPECIES

South of the Arctic Circle, along the length of the great North American continent, live various species of the common, or gray wolf. The most numerous populations and the largest in size are found in Canada and Alaska.

Although there are still a good number of wolves in Minnesota, the population has been greatly reduced. However, in other regions, such as the Rocky Mountains, there is only a very small group left. In the southeast of the United States and the Sierra Madre (Mexico), there is a race of small wolves with light-colored fur. They live in deserted areas and their coloring is reddish brown. They are not to be confused with the red wolf, considered by many to be a different species from the common wolf.

The red wolf is exclusive to North America, and is listed as a species in danger of extinction. It lives in forests and coastal regions in the southeast United States. Previously very numerous, now many consider it already extinct in the wild. It is a small wolf, weighing between 15 and 30 kilograms (33 and 66 pounds). Its fur is shorter than the common wolf and is reddish or cinnamon colored, with black or gray tones. Like the rest of its relations, it is an animal with essentially nocturnal habits. Its habitual prey is otters, water rats, rabbits, deer, and carrion. Given its scarcity its packs are small; barely three or four animals.

In the United States, as in other countries, the wolf has been persecuted and exterminated since time immemorial. The decrease in numbers of wolves has caused the expansion of the coyote, its great competitor.

Right: Gray wolves drinking from a stream, near some elks.

COYOTE

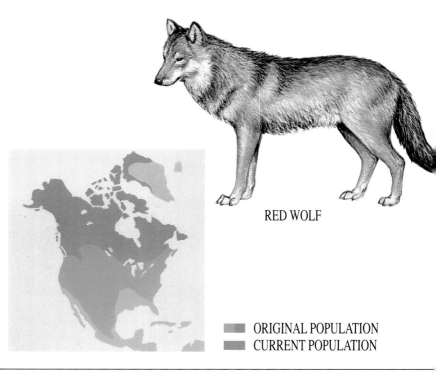

RED WOLF

ORIGINAL POPULATION
CURRENT POPULATION

EUROPE AND ASIA

Although less abundant than in North America, various subspecies also exist in Europe and Asia. Wolves can be found in Arabia, China, Mongolia, India, Russia, Italy, Scandinavia, the Iberian peninsula, and other countries.

Their usual coloring is grayish brown, but there are also wolves that are black, gray or white. In desert regions of some countries of Asia, such as India, Iraq, or northern Arabia, there is a subspecies that is small with reddish fur, the Eurasian red wolf. This is not to be confused with the American red wolf, which, as has been explained earlier, is a different species.

After the bear, the wolf is the largest wild carnivore in Europe. It is not as large as its American cousin, and it lives in forests and mountains. Although it was abundant in the past, its numbers are now small and in many countries, like Britain, Switzerland, or Germany, it has been exterminated. Only in certain countries of the former Soviet Union do populations survive in significant numbers.

The so-called Iberian wolf, which weighs between 25 and 50 kilograms (55 and 110 pounds), is only found in Spain. Its fur is grayish brown and it has characteristic black marks on its forelegs. It only survives in a few small areas and forms very small packs.

Right: In the nineteenth century wolves lived throughout Spain and Portugal. Now they are only found in the northeast and in some parts of the south and southwest—Andalusia and Extremadura.

ARABIAN WOLF

TIBETAN WOLF

HUMANS, A HOSTILE RELATIONSHIP

Fear and hate are the two words that classify the attitude and relationship of humans with wolves. The wolf has been persecuted and exterminated over much of the planet for hundreds of years for its supposed threat to cattle-raising. It is also accused of being a human killer, which is far from the truth.

Hunting and indiscriminate persecution, traps, poison, and progressive industrialization have put these magnificent carnivores in danger. Wolves' numbers have diminished to an alarming extent. Fortunately today the wolf is protected in most countries and in some regions the population is even expanding. However this does not guarantee its future.

The wolf has inspired innumerable legends, stories, and films throughout history. It is present in the imagery and superstitions of many cultures. Generally it is considered a malevolent, diabolical, blood-thirsty creature. It is the protagonist of many horror stories and popular tales, from the werewolf to Little Red Riding Hood. In France the legend of the beast of Gevaudan tells the story of an enormous wolf that killed more than 100 people before being captured.

However in other cultures it has been considered a symbol of power and protection, a divine creature.

Below: Prehistoric man left evidence of the presence of the wolf in the French cave at Font-de-Gaume.

Right: The seventh century figure of a wolf engraved in stone, found in Andross, France.

Left: Not all legends about wolves are negative, such as the well-known legend of Romulus and Remus, the two children nursed by a wolf, who founded Rome; or Mowgli, the wolf-child of India.

Below: A wolf cub feeding from a baby's bottle at a wildlife center.

Right: Many wolves have been exterminated because of the losses they cause to sheep flocks

GLOSSARY

carnivore: An animal that eats meat.

carrion: Rotten meat from a dead animal.

den: Place where animals gather together to sleep and give birth to their young.

dominant: Standing out, in this case the wolf that is stronger than the others.

habitat: Environment in which an animal lives.

herbivore: An animal that feeds on plants.

leader: The one who leads the group.

migration: The regular movement of animals from on place to another, whether for reasons of climate, repro duction, or food.

predator: An animal that hunts others to feed on.

regurgitate: Bring up food from the stomach that h not been digested.

retractable: Capable of being hidden, as in parts of animal's body.

tracks: Footprints, in this case left by the foot of animal.

NDEX